ENGINEERING IN ACTION

ENERGY ENGINEERING
AND Powering the Future

Crabtree Publishing Company

www.crabtreebooks.com

Jonathan Nixon

Crabtree Publishing Company

www.crabtreebooks.com

Author: Jonathan Nixon
Series research and development: Reagan Miller
Editorial director: Kathy Middleton
Photo research: James Nixon
Editors: Paul Humphrey, James Nixon, and
 Philip Gebhardt
Proofreader: Wendy Scavuzzo
Layout: sprout.uk.com
Cover design and logo: Margaret Amy Salter
Production coordinator and prepress technician:
 Margaret Amy Salter
Print coordinator: Katherine Berti

Consultant: Carolyn de Cristofano, M.Ed. STEM
consultant, Professional Development Director of
Engineering is Elementary (2005–2008)

Production coordinated by Discovery Books

Photographs:
Cover: Thinkstock: © George Doyle: (center girl);
 All other images by Shutterstock
Alamy: pp. 4 (ton koene), 6 (imageBROKER), 8 bottom
 (Steve Morgan), 9 (Joerg Boethling), 11 (Cultura
 Creative), 12 top (Jochen Tack), 13 bottom (epa
 european pressphoto agency b.v.), 14 top (Everett
 Collection Historical), 19 (Charlotte Thege), 22 (age
 footstock), 25 bottom (dpa picture alliance archive).
Bigstock: pp. 5 (diro), 7 bottom (Thufir), 8 top (pro6x7),
 15 top (Vincent AF), 16 top (.shock), 17 (olesiabilkei),
 26 (SerrNovik).
Getty Images: pp. 7 top (Tristan Savatier), 10 (Chris
 Ratcliffe/Bloomberg), 12 bottom (Helen H.
 Richardson/The Denver Post), 13 top (TPG), 16 bottom
 (ADEK BERRY/AFP), 20 (John B. Carnett/Bonnier
 Corporation), 21 bottom (Eye Ubiquitous/UIG), 24 top
 (Bobby Longoria).
Shutterstock: p. 21 top (Tewlyx).
Torresol Energy Investments, S.A.: p. 18.
Wikimedia: pp. 7 middle, 14 bottom, 15 middle, 15
 bottom (Blog do Planalto), 23 top (Georgepehli), 23
 middle (Cmglee), 23 bottom (Patrickhaas/cmefe-
 hepia), 24 bottom (Erik Hersman), 25 top, 28 (NASA),
 29 top (Damien Jemison/LLNL), 29 bottom (Sebastien
 Rondet).

Library and Archives Canada Cataloguing in Publication

Nixon, Jonathan, 1986-, author
 Energy engineering and powering the future / Jonathan
Nixon.

(Engineering in action)
Includes index.
Issued in print and electronic formats.
ISBN 978-0-7787-7539-3 (hardback).--
ISBN 978-0-7787-7543-0 (paperback).--
ISBN 978-1-4271-1788-5 (html)

 1. Power (Mechanics)--Juvenile literature. 2. Power
resources--Juvenile literature. 3. Engineering--Juvenile literature.
I. Title. II. Series: Engineering in action (St. Catharines, Ont.)

TJ163.95.N59 2016   j621.042   C2016-903297-3
                                    C2016-903298-1

Library of Congress Cataloging-in-Publication Data

Names: Nixon, Jonathan, 1986- author.
Title: Energy engineering and powering the future / Jonathan
 Nixon.
Description: St Catharines, Ontario ; New York, New York :
 Crabtree Publishing Company, [2016] | Series: Engineering
 in action
Identifiers: LCCN 2016027299 (print) | LCCN 2016029152 (ebook)
 | ISBN 9780778775393 (reinforced library binding : alk. paper)
 | ISBN 9780778775430 (pbk. : alk. paper)
 | ISBN 9781427117885 (Electronic HTML)
Subjects: LCSH: Energy industries--Juvenile literature. | Power
 resources--Juvenile literature. | Renewable energy sources-
 -Juvenile literature. | Sustainable engineering--Juvenile
 literature.
Classification: LCC TJ163.23 .N59 2016 (print) | LCC TJ163.23
 (ebook) | DDC 333.79--dc23
LC record available at https://lccn.loc.gov/2016027299

Crabtree Publishing Company

www.crabtreebooks.com   1-800-387-7650

Printed in Canada/201803/BF20180215

Published in Canada
Crabtree Publishing
616 Welland Ave.
St. Catharines, ON
L2M 5V6

Published in the United States
Crabtree Publishing
PMB 59051
350 Fifth Avenue, 59th Floor
New York, New York 10118

Published in the United Kingdom
Crabtree Publishing
Maritime House
Basin Road North, Hove
BN41 1WR

Published in Australia
Crabtree Publishing
3 Charles Street
Coburg North
VIC, 3058

CONTENTS

WHAT IS ENERGY ENGINEERING?

Energy engineers power the world. They make sure that our demands for energy—electricity, heat, and transportation—are met. They do this by designing and overseeing large- or small-scale energy **systems**. For example, they may work on turning garbage into liquid fuels, operate power stations to generate heat and electricity, or even build mini-suns!

An engineer checks burning garbage in a power station that converts household waste into electricity.

Energy systems need to be affordable and environmentally friendly, so engineers try to make the ways in which we currently work with energy more **efficient** (see page 9). They also carry out research to develop and test new technologies, which can convert natural resources such as wind and coal into useful forms of energy. As populations grow, we need more and more energy. This means energy engineers will play a vital role in our future.

EIGHT STEPS TO SUCCESS

When engineers take on a new energy generation project, they adopt an eight-step process to successfully design, build, and test a solution.

Steps in the design process

Identify the problem

↓

Identify criteria and constraints

↓

Brainstorm ideas

↓

Select a solution

↓

Build a prototype

↺

Improve the design ⟶ Test the prototype

↓

Share the solution

Engineers and scientists: Science and engineering are closely linked. Scientists acquire knowledge about how the world works. Engineers apply that knowledge to develop solutions to problems. For example, a scientist might study a plant to understand how it uses the Sun's energy to grow. An energy engineer may focus on ways to convert the energy stored within a plant into usable energy, such as heat, electricity, or fuels for vehicles.

FORMS OF ENERGY

Energy engineers work with different forms of energy to supply our daily needs. These forms include:

- Kinetic energy: The movement of something, such as the wind or waves
- Potential energy: The energy stored in an object due to its position. For example, raising an object creates **gravitational potential energy** and stretching a rubber band results in **elastic potential energy**
- Thermal energy: The energy that comes from heat
- Chemical energy: Energy stored in food, fuels, and batteries
- Radiant energy: For example, light from the Sun, which is also known as solar energy
- Nuclear energy: The energy stored in the nuclei (the central part) of **atoms**
- Sound energy: Energy caused by vibrating objects
- Electrical energy: For example, electricity or a bolt of lightning

Energy engineers develop systems, such as **electrical grids**, to transport energy. Electrical grids need to withstand bad weather such as lightning.

WORKING WITH ENERGY

Even though we see and interact with energy every day (when cooking, traveling, and watching television), we cannot create energy. Instead, energy is converted from one form to another form. For example, electrical energy is converted into heat in an oven, or sound and light in a television. Energy engineers design solutions for converting forms of energy into the electricity we use. But where does the energy they work with come from?

*The Sun warms Earth unevenly, which causes the wind to blow. Energy engineers use wind **turbines** to convert this wind energy into electricity.*

Energy flow

Most of the energy available to us originates from the Sun. For example, plants absorb solar energy so that they can grow. **Fossil fuels**, such as coal and oil, are the ancient remains of plants and other life forms. They still store energy that originally came from the Sun millions of years ago. When industries burn fossil fuels, this chemical energy is released as thermal (heat) energy.

Energy engineers can use thermal energy in devices called **engines**. In an engine, some form of energy—often thermal—is used to make a shaft rotate. This rotation is a form of mechanical energy, which is a combination of potential energy and kinetic energy. Mechanical energy can be used in different ways, such as to power a car. By connecting an engine's rotating shaft to a **generator**, mechanical energy can also be turned into electrical energy. In physics, we call the process of transferring energy "work." The rate at which work is performed or, in this case, at which electrical energy is converted from mechanical energy, is called power.

NICOLAS LÉONARD SADI CARNOT

Thermodynamics is an area of physics that focuses on how thermal energy can be changed into other energy forms. In 1824, Nicolas Léonard Sadi Carnot, a French engineer, calculated the maximum amount of work that could be obtained from an engine using thermal energy. This became known as the Carnot Cycle, which defines the "perfect" engine. Today, Nicolas Carnot is referred to as the "father of thermodynamics."

Nuclear engineering: In addition to the Sun's energy, engineers can also harness nuclear energy on Earth. Nuclear energy is what keeps Earth's interior hot. We can mine nuclear materials to make use of the energy they store. For example, uranium is a nuclear material that contains highly concentrated amounts of energy and, when **refined**, energy engineers use it as a fuel in nuclear power stations, submarines, and even spacecraft.

Engineers use nuclear energy to power submarines so that they can stay underwater for long periods.

FINDING A BETTER WAY

Fossil fuels are an important source of energy for the world. The fuels store large amounts of energy. However, fossil fuels take a very long time to form, so they are considered to be **non-renewable**. Eventually we will run out of fossil fuels, so energy engineers have to devise ways to use them as efficiently as possible. There is another major problem with using fossil fuels. **Carbon dioxide** is formed when fossil fuels are burned. This is causing the planet to warm and the global climate to change.

Coal-fired power plants produce 41 percent of the global supply of electricity. However, they pollute the air and contribute to climate change.

Sustainability is the idea of meeting our current energy needs without reducing the ability for future generations to meet theirs. Renewable energy is energy from a resource that is replaced as quickly as it is used, such as sunlight. Renewable energy can be costly, so energy engineers are trying to find renewable solutions that are as effective and inexpensive as fossil fuels.

Engineers test a new floating device that makes electricity from the movement of the sea's tides. Tidal power is a form of renewable energy that is more predictable than wind power or solar power.

DEVELOPING ENERGY

Wealthy countries have been using fossil fuels for a long time and this has contributed to climate change. **Developing countries** use less energy per person, but their yearly demands are increasing very quickly. Energy is particularly important for developing countries because it is needed for tackling **poverty**. Industries need energy to expand. Energy is also needed to harvest and preserve food, as well as to provide clean drinking water. The problem is that some of the world's poorest countries are being harmed the most by climate change. Long, dry periods and expanding deserts are making it harder to grow food, while rising sea levels will result in people having to leave their homes.

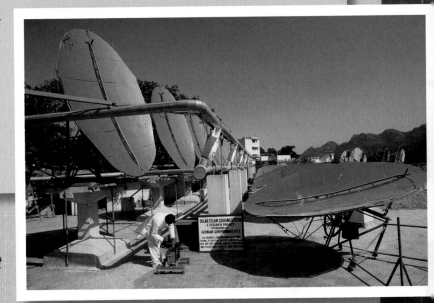

In Rajasthan, India, engineers have designed and made a system that uses curved mirrors to focus sunlight and produce heat for cooking.

Increasing efficiency: When energy is converted from one form into another form, some energy is wasted. Energy engineers try to make systems and devices more efficient by reducing this waste. **Friction**, caused by surfaces moving against each other, is a big problem. It causes the engine of a car to be noisy and get hot. These are ways in which energy is lost. Engineers can try to reduce friction by using smoother components, and by designing shapes that are more streamlined. For example, engineers are exploring the possibility of covering wind turbine blades in a super-thin and slippery covering called a nano-coating. Reducing the amount of energy that is wasted means money can be saved. It will also help to protect the environment.

FOSSIL AND NUCLEAR POWER

Coal, oil, and natural gas, and more recently nuclear, are the main energy sources used today to produce heat and power. Some power stations are huge, such as the world's largest coal-fired power station in Taichung, Taiwan. There, ships bring 14.5 million tons (13 million metric tons) of coal every year from around the globe. Approximately 80 percent of the world's energy needs are met by fossil fuels, so energy engineers can make an enormous difference if they focus on improving fossil-fueled power stations.

Capturing heat

To improve the efficiency of power stations, energy engineers are trying to find ways to minimize or capture any heat losses—caused by friction, for example. In a **combined cycle power plant**, gas is burned to fuel an engine and produce electricity. The heat loss from the engine is then captured and used to create steam. The steam can then be used to turn a turbine, which is a special type of engine that has a spinning shaft fitted with blades like a fan. When the turbine is connected to a generator, more electricity can be produced.

An engineer checks that a steam turbine is ready to be installed in a power station.

Engineers in control rooms monitor nuclear power stations very closely.

NUCLEAR HAZARD

Using nuclear power to generate electricity doesn't release carbon dioxide into the atmosphere. However, there are other major hazards. The process creates highly **radioactive** waste. If accidents occur, harmful amounts of nuclear **radiation** can be released. When designing nuclear power stations, energy engineers need to include many safety systems in their designs. Teams of engineers design technologies that can filter radiation out of the air and stand firm against natural disasters such as earthquakes. Sometimes they have to develop solutions to problems after something has already gone wrong.

In 1986, a catastrophic nuclear disaster occurred at Chernobyl Nuclear Power Station in Ukraine. A power surge caused the plant to explode, releasing dangerous radioactive material into the air. Engineers encased the plant in concrete, but in 2016, they had to cover it again, this time by building the world's largest human-made movable structure. The area around Chernobyl is so dangerous that no one is allowed to live within 18 miles (30 km) of the plant for the next 20,000 years! In 2011, Fukushima Nuclear Power Station in Japan suffered major damage from an earthquake and a huge wave called a tsunami. Engineers proposed the solution: A wall of ice is now being built around the plant to stop radiation from leaking out.

ENGINEERING RENEWABLES

The main sources of renewable energy that engineers harness are solar, wind, hydro (flowing water), **biomass**, and geothermal (heat from the ground). These sources can be used in different ways. For example, sunlight can be focused using lenses or mirrors to generate lots of heat. Sunlight can be converted directly into electricity through **photovoltaic panels** (solar panels), which you often see on the roofs of houses.

A biomass power plant burns large amounts of wood to make heat and electricity.

Energy from crops

Biomass, such as woodchips and food crops, is of particular interest to energy engineers. It can be burned to heat homes, converted into biofuels to run cars, and used in large quantities to feed power stations. However, there is more energy per ton stored in fossil fuels such as coal, so a lot of biomass is needed to provide the same amount of power. Some farmland is now used to grow crops for biofuels instead of food. This has raised concerns because there are already food shortages in some parts of the world.

This rickshaw vehicle in Thailand is powered by animal waste from a zoo!

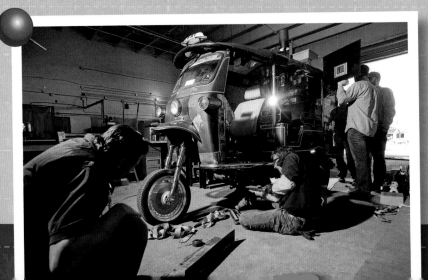

BIGGER AND BIGGER

Energy engineers are continuously making energy systems larger to try to achieve gains in output and efficiency. Power used by home appliances such as toasters, kettles, and hair dryers, is measured in watts. The power generated by a power station may be measured in megawatts (a million watts) or gigawatts (a billion watts).

- The Three Gorges Dam in China is a 22.5-gigawatt (GW) **hydroelectric power** station. Here, water is drained to rush through 32 turbines linked to electric generators. It is the world's largest power station, and it took 18 years for engineers to fully complete!

Water rushes through The Three Gorges Dam hydroelectric power station in China.

- Ivanpah Solar Electric Generating System, in California's Mojave Desert, is a 392-megawatt (MW) solar-thermal power plant. It uses 173,500 mirrors to focus the Sun's energy and turn water into steam. The steam drives turbines that produce electricity.

- Drax Power Station in England is converting half of its plant to use biomass instead of coal. It will need more than 8 million tons (7.5 million metric tons) of biomass every year to generate 1.3 GW of power.

- The Vestas V164 8-MW wind turbine, built in 2014 in Denmark, is 722 feet (220 m) tall and the largest in the world. Each rotating turbine blade is over 328 feet (100 m) long!

A prototype of one of the world's longest wind turbine blades is lifted by a crane.

THE HISTORY OF ENERGY ENGINEERING

Edison's power station used six generators and could power 1,100 light bulbs.

As far back as ancient times, humans have burned wood for heat, and made simple water and wind mechanisms to process food grain. However, it was around the time of **The Industrial Revolution**, in the 18th and 19th centuries, that the craze for coal began. Engineers, such as Scottish inventor James Watt, designed steam engines powered by coal, which could run large factories. Engineers soon discovered how to use an engine's motion to make electricity. In 1882, Thomas Edison built the world's first coal-fired power station in New York, which provided heat and lighting to Manhattan.

For his contribution to science and engineering, Charles Parsons was knighted by the British king in 1911.

The engine: The engine—a device for converting a form of energy into mechanical work—dates back to the 3rd century, when water was first used to power a **sawmill**. It was not until the 1600s that the first fuel-burning engine was developed. Energy from burning gunpowder was used to drive a water pump. It was soon replaced by the steam engine. Then, in 1884, British engineer Sir Charles Parsons invented the modern steam turbine—a more efficient engine for power generation. Today, steam turbines provide approximately 80 percent of the world's electricity.

In the past, engineers used windmills to grind grain and to pump water. Unlike wind turbines, windmills don't produce electricity.

THE FIRST ENERGY ENGINEER?

Hero of Alexandria was a Greek mathematician and engineer who wrote about the inventions he created during the 1st century c.e. Among his many inventions was a musical organ operated by a windmill. Hero also designed a simple steam engine. When placed over a fire, steam spurted out of two pipes, causing a ball to rotate (above right.) At the time, there was no application for his engine, so Hero displayed it in temples to amaze people.

Toward cleaner energy

By the early 1900s, coal-fired power stations were commonplace. The invention of the steam turbine and low-cost cars further accelerated the demand for fossil fuels. It was not until the 1970s that people began to worry about fossil fuels. During this period, there was a limited supply of oil and the cost of fossil fuels increased. Several years later, a far more serious problem started to emerge. Our use of fossil fuels was warming the planet—with potentially disastrous effects. In response, leaders from around the world gathered in 1992 at the Earth Summit held in Rio de Janeiro, Brazil, and agreed to work together for the first time to combat climate change.

This spurred engineers to focus on the development of renewable and cleaner energy solutions.

World leaders met in Rio de Janeiro again for the 20th anniversary of the Earth Summit, to ensure that progress toward cleaner energy was being made.

TODAY'S ENERGY ENGINEER

Energy engineers work on all kinds of different projects. As an energy engineer, you might end up designing wind turbines, developing computer programs to control solar energy systems, or managing a nuclear power station. Since the field is so broad, energy engineers normally specialize on a particular technology, such as photovoltaics, geothermal energy, or nuclear energy.

An engineer monitors newly installed photovoltaic panels to make sure that they are working as efficiently as possible.

While some universities do offer degrees in energy engineering, many energy engineers pursue studies in related fields, such as chemical, mechanical, automotive, civil, or aerospace engineering.

Students interested in pursuing a career in energy engineering typically require a strong background in math and physics. However, energy engineers need to develop other skills. They need to be good at conducting research, solving problems, working in a team, and communicating ideas effectively.

An engineer works at a geothermal power station that has been designed to capture the thermal energy stored beneath a volcano!

I AM AN ENERGY ENGINEER

Mary Gillie is an energy engineer who started out studying for a degree in physics. Mary didn't know she wanted to be an engineer at first. It was her desire to do something that she viewed as useful that attracted her to the field of renewable energy. Studying physics had developed her problem-solving skills, and given her a basic understanding of engineering. She went on to complete a **doctorate** in control engineering, which focused on modeling the performance of wind turbines. Mary then worked as an energy **consultant,** where she found ways to supply renewable energy to electrical grids. Later, Mary decided she wanted to focus on improving how we use energy. She now runs a company that helps people make their homes more energy efficient.

Working together: Before implementing an energy system, many environmental checks need to be performed. For example, when a dam is built for a hydroelectric power station, an engineer will determine how big it needs to be and how much power can be produced. Scientists might investigate how the water quality will be affected and how surrounding wildlife might be harmed. Based on the scientists' findings, engineers may decide to come up with a new project proposal, such as a smaller system or an alternative location. By working together, engineers and scientists try to minimize any negative environmental impact.

Scientists who study weather patterns, and energy engineers who design wind turbines, work together to determine a suitable site for a wind farm.

MEETING THE CHALLENGE

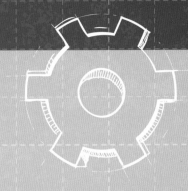

Energy engineers are always striving to improve the way we use and convert energy. At the start of any new project, the first task is to clearly identify the goals to be achieved. Energy engineers then have to define the constraints within which possible solutions must operate.

The problem: Energy engineering projects are developed to address particular problems. For example, many remote areas of Africa do not have access to electricity. Electricity is needed to power pumps that bring much-needed water up from underground. Another problem energy engineers face is how to provide renewable sources of energy, night and day, all the year round. It is not always sunny and the wind is not always blowing.

24/7 SOLAR POWER

Engineers at Gemasolar in Spain use mirrors that focus sunlight onto a single point to create very high temperatures.

Making a large solar power station work when it is dark is a challenge. To overcome this problem, engineers are trying to store some of the Sun's energy during the day so it can be used at night. At Gemasolar power station in Seville, Spain, engineers had the idea to store the Sun's energy in molten (melted) salt. At night, the hot salt is used to turn water into steam. During the summer, the power station can generate electricity all day and all night, purely using solar energy!

Criteria and constraints: Every project has certain specifications that must be met. A specification could be that the solution has to provide one megawatt of power. There will also be constraints, which limit the solution, such as a maximum size or the maximum amount of fuel that can be used. Criteria are things by which designs can be judged and compared. For example, different solar-powered water pumps would be judged on how much water they provide or how much they cost. Engineers often have to make a compromise between performance and cost. This is known as a **trade-off**.

WATER FOR AFRICA

SCL Water is a company that specializes in providing water solutions to rural areas of Africa. Recently, their engineers faced the challenge of pumping an uninterrupted supply of clean water to two Ugandan villages, located more than 500 yards (0.5 km) apart. A constraint was that the solution had to work without any human operation. Their solution was to create a single well, located between the two villages, and use photovoltaic panels to power water pumps. Because the photovoltaic panels would not work at night, they placed a large tank on the roof of a nearby building and used the pumps to fill it with water during the day. Lifting water up into the air is a way of storing the Sun's energy as gravitational potential energy. When a faucet is opened at night, **gravity** causes the water to flow to the village.

In remote areas of Africa, solar energy can be used to power water pumps.

POSSIBLE SOLUTIONS

A major step in all projects is the generation of ideas. Using these ideas, a design can be chosen and a prototype can be built.

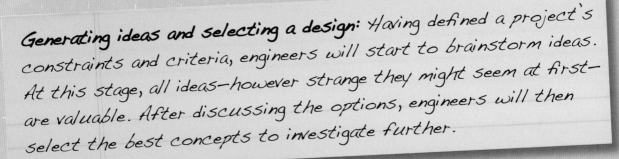

Generating ideas and selecting a design: Having defined a project's constraints and criteria, engineers will start to brainstorm ideas. At this stage, all ideas—however strange they might seem at first—are valuable. After discussing the options, engineers will then select the best concepts to investigate further.

Crazy or what?

In the 1970s, energy engineers had the idea of having wind turbines floating out at sea where there is more wind. Given that wind turbines can be the height of skyscrapers, this seemed ridiculous at first. However, by the 1990s, engineers started to take the idea seriously. High up in the atmosphere, the wind is even stronger. So energy engineers are now developing ideas for wind turbines that can fly!

American inventor Doug Selsam tests a prototype of his wind turbine, which would be held up at high altitudes by a balloon. He calls it the Sky Serpent!

Building models: The most common way that engineers evaluate their ideas is to develop prototypes. Prototypes are important because they enable potential flaws and problems to be identified before a design is finalized. To investigate the idea of a flying wind turbine, energy engineers have built prototypes that consist of **helium**-filled balloons and huge kites.

BRAINSTORMERS

Scotsman James Blyth was the first energy engineer to experiment with wind turbines to make electricity. His earliest prototypes consisted of fabric sails and large bowl-shaped boxes to rotate machinery and charge batteries. However, they worked too well, spinning so fast that they destroyed themselves in strong winds. Blyth didn't give up. By the late 1880s, he had a much better design and was able to light his home using wind power. His house became the first in the world to be powered by electricity from the wind.

In 1931, French engineer Georges Jean Marie Darrieus developed ideas so that wind turbines didn't have to face the wind to work. Unlike most designs, his wind turbines used curved blades and had a vertical rotating shaft. His work led to a design now known as the Darrieus wind turbine, and the tallest wind turbine of this type is still in operation today in Quebec, Canada.

Over the years, energy engineers have played around with many different wind turbine designs.

The world's largest Darrieus wind turbine is located on the Gaspé Peninsula in Cap-Chat, Quebec, Canada.

TESTING, TESTING

Once a prototype has been made, it must be tested. Testing reveals flaws in an engineer's design. Designs are then modified before a final—and possibly expensive—product is made.

Physical and simulation testing: Energy engineers use many methods to test their designs. They may try to see how much force it takes to break a prototype. This is known as destructive testing. This type of testing can be expensive, so **simulations** are performed on computers instead. For example, computer modeling lets engineers simulate how water will flow through a dam in a hydroelectric power station. After evaluating the results from the tests, engineers may need to refine their designs.

Energy engineers can use computer programs to test their designs.

Improving the design: The process of testing prototypes, refining designs, building new prototypes, and carrying out more tests is repeated in a cycle. During testing, engineers sometimes discover that they need to develop completely new ideas. Once an engineer is completely satisfied with the design, a final product can be manufactured.

Fluid flows

Engineers are particularly interested in learning how fluids (liquids and gases) flow over their designs. They can do this by observing fast-flowing air in large **wind tunnels** or by simulating fluid flows on computers. Smoke and lasers can also be used in wind tunnels to help engineers see how flowing air behaves. Knowledge of how fluids flow over turbine blades allows energy engineers to refine their simulations and designs so that they can increase the power obtained from the wind, steam, or rushing water.

When designing a wind turbine to be installed on a building, it is important to simulate how the wind flows over and around that building. By doing this, engineers will know where to position the turbine so it catches the most wind possible.

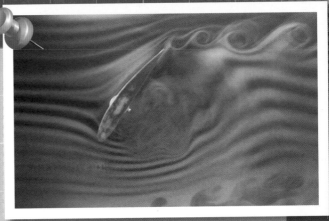

Fog is one way to visualize the flow of air over a design in a wind tunnel.

The wind turbines on the Strata Tower in London rarely spin because they are poorly positioned.

WEATHER-PROOFING

Before finalizing a design, engineers test how strong winds might affect the performance of their energy systems. They may conduct wind tunnel tests on full-scale models to investigate how the wind will bend and move photovoltaic panels, for example. Sometimes things go wrong once a product has been finalized. The curved mirrors used in solar power stations are expensive, but they are fragile and can break. The National Renewable Energy Laboratory in Colorado used smoke and small-scale models to learn how the wind was flowing over the mirrors, so that design improvements could be made and costly damage reduced.

The performance and durability of a prototype wind turbine can be tested in a wind tunnel.

SHARING SOLUTIONS

Sharing solutions and the knowledge gained from projects is an important part of energy engineering. Sometimes it enables scientific breakthroughs to be made many years later, and sharing stories of failures allows engineers to learn important lessons from past mistakes. To do this effectively, engineers will publish their work in scientific **journals** or books, present their findings at conferences, and give lectures at universities.

A STORY ABOUT JUNK

Self-taught engineers have shared their work, too. In 2002, William Kamkwamba—an out-of-school teen living in poverty in Malawi—engineered a wind turbine using wood from local trees and parts from a junkyard. He used the wind turbine to power electrical appliances in his home. He shared his story by publishing a book called The Boy Who Harnessed the Wind. Kamkwamba has presented his work at many conferences, and was featured in a documentary film. He has since used solar power to provide drinking water to his village.

William Kamkwamba talks about his work at a festival in Texas in 2013.

William Kamkwamba's wind turbine included scrap parts from a bicycle and a tractor! The turbine is located on a tower built using wood from gum trees.

24

EINSTEIN'S PAPERS

Engineers learn from each other's papers, as well as from scientists' papers. Albert Einstein (1879-1955) shared his work by publishing hundreds of scientific papers during his life. At the time, most of his work was not understood, but one of his papers set humans on the path to discovering nuclear power and another led to the development of photovoltaic panels.

Albert Einstein works on his papers at the University of Berlin, Germany.

The hazards of energy: Even though engineers hope to solve many energy-related problems with newer technologies, these technologies also come with challenges. Engineers and scientists have recently learned that some biofuels are potentially more harmful to the environment than fossil fuels. This is because some crops require **fertilizers** to grow and use a lot of energy to be converted into fuel. At biomass plants, there have been several fires due to the biomass **spontaneously combusting!** Solar power stations and wind turbines can get too hot and catch fire if they are not carefully controlled. Making energy cleanly and safely is an ongoing problem, but energy engineers will continue to share their work so improvements can be made.

A wind turbine catches fire due to a faulty generator.

DESIGN CHALLENGE

Now it's time to use the eight-step design process to develop an energy-efficient windmill for turning kinetic energy into useful mechanical power. You may wish to work with a friend or in a group, so you can share ideas and learn from each other.

The suggested materials and equipment for this design-and-make challenge are:

- One or two large plastic bottles (for the tower)

- String

- Scissors

- Bag of marbles

- Paper or card stock

- Tape

- Pins

- Plastic straws, pencils (or similar)

1. The problem: The challenge is to design, build, and test a windmill that is capable of lifting a small bag of marbles (or something of a similar mass). Well-designed windmills will be able to lift more marbles (do more work). By increasing the speed of lift (the rate at which work is done) for a certain mass, the more power you will have achieved.

2. Criteria and constraints: Develop a list of criteria to compare and assess your designs. For example, what is the maximum number of marbles your windmill can lift? Other criteria to use are strength, reliability, and efficiency. Wastage is important, too. Therefore, when you build your design, take note of how much material you use and how much goes to waste (e.g., scrap paper or plastic). Set yourself some constraints. These might include a maximum budget, or the time allowed to build your windmill.

3. Brainstorm: What ideas can you think of? Come up with several. For example, you could try using different numbers of blades or different shapes. Think about how you will attach the blades, and the marbles (mass), to a rotating shaft. Make some sketches to jot down your ideas.

4. Select a design: Select your most promising design based on the initial problem and the criteria and constraints for the solution.

5. Build a prototype: Make a final detailed drawing of your design, then make a working prototype. The prototype should be fully operational, but don't worry about getting things perfect at this stage.

6. Test the prototype: Use an electric fan to test how well the prototype works. Are there problems? What is causing the problems? Is the windmill stable? Are the blades durable and stiff enough? If you are using a fan with multiple speed settings, how does the windmill perform in high and low winds? Can your windmill lift even more marbles? Repeat your tests to make sure that your system is reliable.

7. Improve the design: Think about how you could refine your design to improve its performance. Could the blades be larger or fitted more securely? Perhaps fewer materials could be used, or maybe the tower could be filled with water or sand to make it more stable. Can you increase the windmill's efficiency? This would involve increasing the windmill's power without increasing the wind speed or blade length.

8. Share your work: Keep a record of your designs and results. Present your work to friends or family. Tell them about any changes you made to your designs after testing. Include clear diagrams and instructions, so that your work could be recreated.

A CLEAN FUTURE

Energy engineers will design systems that use coal, oil, and gas for many more years. However, engineers are seeking ways to ensure fossil fuels cause less harm to the environment. For example, they are investigating how to capture the carbon dioxide that is released when fossil fuels are burned. This captured carbon can be stored deep underground or below the oceans, and will be prevented from contributing to climate change.

ENERGY FROM SPACE

In the future, electricity could be sent wirelessly to Earth from space. Organizations such as the Japanese Space Agency and NASA have been investigating a concept known as space-based solar power. In space, the Sun's energy is stronger and there can be no night time. Satellites make use of photovoltaic panels to capture and convert solar energy into electricity, but the challenge is beaming the electrical energy down to Earth!

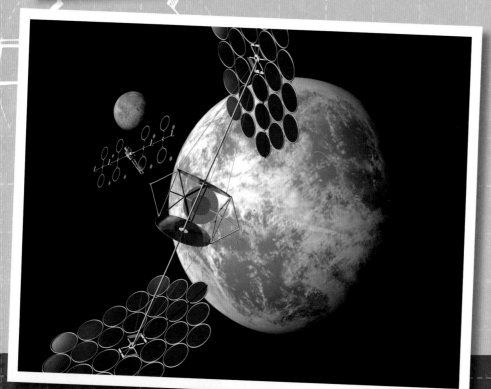

NASA has been working on concepts for space-based solar power since the 1970s. One idea is a large inflatable satellite system that could beam more than a gigawatt of power down to Earth.

BUILDING A SUN

Engineers have been trying to recreate the power of the Sun on Earth. The Joint European Torus system located in the UK is a fusion **reactor** that mimics the nuclear reactions in the Sun. In the system, two **hydrogen** atoms are heated to 180 million degrees Fahrenheit (100 million degrees Celsius) and fused together. Huge amounts of energy are released during the fusion process, and the fused atoms are so hot that giant magnets have to prevent any contact with the reactor walls.

The idea is that energy could be used to make electricity in the future. The National Ignition Facility (NIF) in California is a similar system, which uses the world's largest laser to heat and fuse hydrogen atoms.

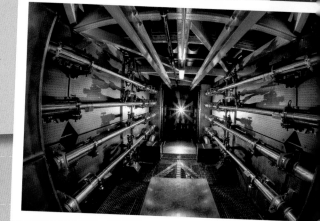

The NIF recently achieved a 500,000 gigawatt flash of light. This is a thousand times more power than the United States uses at any one moment.

Future transportation: It is likely that most transportation will eventually be powered by cleaner and renewable resources. Improvements in batteries will lead to electric cars becoming more common. Engineers and scientists have even managed to turn food waste and garbage into liquid fuels, which could be used to power airplanes and cars. Hydrogen is already being used to fuel a handful of buses in some cities, and in the state of California, there are several public hydrogen refueling stations.

Energy engineers will continue working on these and other projects to help us build safe and sustainable energy systems for the future.

Engineers at Jaguar have designed an electric car that uses two small gas turbines to charge its batteries.

LEARNING MORE

BOOKS

Kamkwamba, William, and Bryan Mealer. *The Boy Who Harnessed the Wind: Creating Currents of Electricity and Hope*. William Morrow, 2010.

Raum, Elizabeth. *Fossil Fuels and Biofuels* (Fueling the Future). Heinemann Library, 2008.

Snedden, Robert. *Environmental Engineering and the Science of Sustainability* (Engineering in Action). Crabtree Publishing, 2014.

Sneideman, Joshua, and Erin Twamley. *Renewable Energy: Discover the Fuel of the Future with 20 Projects*. Nomad Press, 2016.

Spilsbury, Richard. *Fossil Fuel Power (Lets Discuss Energy Resources)*. PowerKids Press, 2011.

ONLINE

www.childrensuniversity.manchester. ac.uk/interactives/science/energy
Learn more about energy through some interactive videos here.

www.alliantenergykids.com/ FunandGames/OnlineGames
Test your knowledge of energy and the environment by playing these games.

www.eia.gov/kids/energy. cfm?page=renewable_home-basics
Learn more about how renewable energy is used.

www.kids.esdb.bg/index.html
Find out more about energy here.

www.2025labs.com/energy
Search this site to learn more about engineering and energy.

PLACES TO VISIT

The Museum of Science and Industry, Chicago, Illinois
www.msichicago.org
One of the world's largest museums, with much to discover about all things science and engineering.

Ontario Science Centre, Toronto
www.ontariosciencecentre.ca
This museum has some great exhibits for kids.

GLOSSARY

atoms Tiny particles from which all materials are made

biomass Material made up of dead or living organisms that is used as a fuel

carbon dioxide A colorless gas made of carbon and oxygen

combined cycle power plant A system that combines a gas engine and a steam turbine

consultant A professional person who provides expert advice

developing countries Countries with relatively low incomes and underdeveloped industries

doctorate The highest degree awarded by a university

efficient Achieving maximum productivity with minimal wasted effort or expense

elastic potential energy Energy stored in a stretched object such as an elastic band

electrical grid An energy system for transporting electricity

engine A machine with moving parts that converts forms of energy into motion

fertilizer A substance to help plants and food crops grow

fossil fuels Material that originated from the remains of dead organisms, which have been buried for millions of years and which can be burned to release energy

friction A force that resists the movement of surfaces sliding against each other

generator A device for converting mechanical energy into electricity

gravitational potential energy Energy stored in a raised object due to gravity

gravity A force that attracts objects to each other due to their mass

helium A gas that is the second lightest chemical element

hydroelectric power Electricity obtained from flowing water

hydrogen A gas and the lightest chemical element; hydrogen is the most abundant substance in the universe

journal A magazine in which professionals who are focused on a particular field share information and the results of their work

non-renewable Cannot be replaced once it is used up

photovoltaic panels A technology that converts solar energy directly into electrical energy

poverty The lack of possessions or money

prototype An early model for testing a design or concept

radiation Energy released in the form of particles and waves, which can be dangerous to human health

radioactive Gives off radiation

reactor A containment system in which chemical or nuclear reactions are controlled

refined Has had any impurities removed

sawmill A building that uses mechanical energy for sawing wood

simulation Using a model to imitate a real-world process

spontaneously combusting Catching fire by itself

system A combination of parts and/or processes that work together

The Industrial Revolution A period of time (around 1760-1840) when industries started to use water and steam to power machines, and new manufacturing methods were developed

trade-off A compromise between desirable, but incompatible, criteria

turbine A device with blades that is made to spin by flowing liquids or gases

wind tunnel A tunnel in which a stream of air is produced to test the effects of wind on models and full-sized objects

INDEX